Give It Up!™

Stop smoking for life.

by

Anne Mitchell

Foreword by

Daniel James Hudson

President and CEO, Arbor Int. Inc.

Dipl. Ac. NCCAOM

Alyeska
Press, LLC

Give It Up!™
Stop smoking for life.

Published 2002 by **Alyeska Press, LLC**
1153 Bergen Parkway, Suite M, PMB #275, Evergreen, CO 80439
www.alyeskapress.com

Printed and bound in the United States of America using
recycled paper and soy inks.

Book design and cover photography by Anne Mitchell.
Author photograph by Cynthia B. Russell.

Give It Up! is a trademark of Alyeska Press, LLC.
ZYBAN is a registered trademark of Glaxo Wellcome Inc.
Benefits of quitting smoking source: the American Cancer
Society, Inc. Used with permission.

Mitchell, Anne, 1959-.
        Give It Up! Stop smoking for life.
        Includes reading recommendations, references, and
        index. Audio CD accompanies book and is not to be
        sold separately.

        Library of Congress Control Number: 2002090530
        ISBN 0-9711600-0-7

        1. Health
        2. Self-help techniques
        3. Cigarette smoking–Rehabilitation
        4. Tobacco habit–Treatment

This book/CD may be ordered in quantity at a discount
off the cover price (see order form in back of book). Contact the
publisher for special sales or bulk-order pricing and for information on
copublishing opportunities, or go to www.alyeskapress.com.

Give It Up!™

Stop smoking for life.

CONTENTS

Dedication i

Foreword iii

Acknowledgments vii

Introduction 1

Part One: Beyond the Smoke Screen

Why you smoke 13

How smoking hurts you 29

Part Two: Gaining Clarity

The benefits of quitting 47

A vision for you 53

Part Three: Give It Up!

Stop smoking for life 67

The stories 77

The speakers 81

CONTENTS

Part Four: Woman to Woman

    Recent findings 87

    Tomorrow's victims 89

    Could be hazardous 99

    The target is you 105

    Realities of quitting 117

Part Five: Staying With It

    Tips from ex-smokers 125

    It all adds up 135

    In closing 143

Recommended reading 147

Web sites of interest 149

References 153

Index 157

DEDICATION

With gratitude and devotion, I dedicate this book to my friends and family who patiently loved and supported me as I struggled to find freedom from my addictions.

To Roxie Speer, my good friend and partner in crime; to Lisa Reid, my loving sister and best friend; to Michael and Matthew, my sweet, not-so-little brothers; to my parents, Kirsten and Paul McVey, who were there for me when I needed them; to my husband Robert, who showed me what freedom looked like; and to my beautiful daughter Cassidy, who is my constant joy and inspiration.

My heart goes out to those who have suffered from the effects of this deadly addiction and to their families and loved ones.

And a word of comfort for the smoker who so desperately wants to stop being a smoker: There is hope.

———

FOREWORD

An acupuncturist and herbalist since 1994, Daniel James Hudson has extensive experience with addictions and substance abuse. He has trained with doctors from around the world in the areas of traditional Chinese medicine and homeopathy.

Anne Mitchell, in her long and arduous journey to become a nonsmoker, has created what I believe to be one of the finest tools available in the arena of smoking-cessation aids on the market to date.

This tool includes staggering facts about smoking and its effects, the all-important tips that aid in one's road to recovery, and an absolutely compelling audio CD. Anne employs a unique touch of realism and sheer honesty in her approach to the tobacco industry, nicotine addiction, and how to be free from its shackles.

I have personally treated a multitude of addicted smokers using various methods, from acupuncture and herbs to homeopathy and essential oils, with a relatively high percentage of success. It is my belief that had my patients had this tool at their disposal, our success rate would have easily jumped to between 95 and 100 percent. That being said, I would personally recommend this book and CD not only to individuals who are seeking help with their goal to quit smoking, but to those professionals whose job it is to help facilitate this process as well.

In conclusion, *Give It Up! Stop smoking for life* is an informative guide, teacher, friend, and support group all in one, and I predict that it will transform you. I take great pleasure in welcoming you to your new life as a nonsmoker.

Daniel James Hudson

President and CEO, Arbor Int. Inc.

Dipl. Ac. NCCAOM

ACKNOWLEDGMENTS

Having never written a book before, this has been quite a learning experience. In addition to the book, there was a recording to produce and a Web site to build. To make it even more interesting, I had made the decision to self-publish. This was done so that I could retain full creative control and make sure it got to press in a timely fashion. Little did I know how little I knew! Somehow this project still managed to see the light of day, but only because of the contributions of many kind and helpful people.

Some people volunteered on a very personal basis by agreeing to be interviewed for the recording. Others contributed by reading my early manuscripts and giving me input and encouragement. Some were helpful just by being my friends and not questioning my sanity when in fact they had every reason to do so. I will attempt to thank everyone here for their part in this project, and I hope that I have not forgotten anyone.

For their honesty and willingness to bare their hearts and share their hopes, my gratitude and respect go to Denise Becker, Joe Cerullo, Greg Marko, Terri Robinson, Courtney Speer, Robyn Speer, Roxie Speer, and Jen Wallis.*

For his exceptional musical talent and his ability to improvise and come up with just the

*Some names have been changed to protect privacy.

right sound, my thanks go to Ken Rowe. His tranquil background music made the recording really come together.

Randy Hansen of Fanfare Productions was most patient and helpful during the entire recording and sound-editing process. His technical expertise combined with his sensitivity to and understanding of the project were instrumental to its success.

For giving me feedback, advice, and support, I thank John Moyers, Sarah Herold, JR Hayden, Mark Nichols, and Lana Stamato.

For her sound publishing advice and her extreme helpfulness, my thanks go to Polly Wirtz from Peak Consulting.

For their patient and professional assistance with various legal and accounting matters, I thank Fred Wells of The Wells Law Firm; Shelly Rowan of Cohen & Silverman; and Barbara Scripps of Scripps & Associates.

ACKNOWLEDGMENTS

Using not only her wonderful editing skills, but also her experience as an ex-smoker, I again have to thank Jen Wallis. Her ability to clean up my writing without changing my message is priceless.

Six teenage girls gave up a long afternoon this past spring to participate in a focus group during which they shared their insights and experiences related to smoking. They are Robyn and Courtney Speer, Diana and Kirsten Martin, Danielle Garnett, and Jennifer Hollingsworth. Their refreshingly candid talk helped me to better understand today's young female smoker, and I am grateful for their time and their enthusiastic cooperation.

Special thanks go to Daniel Hudson for his generous contribution of time and professional expertise. His unique perspective helped open my eyes to a whole new way of looking at things.

Years ago, a friend named Toni Bertman told me that I had a talent for the English language and

ACKNOWLEDGMENTS

that maybe I should be a writer someday. I never forgot her words and have held the idea close to my heart all of these years. Thank you, Toni.

And finally, I want to thank the American Cancer Society for their online support group for cancer survivors and for the very helpful volunteers I encountered while researching this book. Since money is still much needed for cancer research, support, and education, I have decided to donate a percentage of this project's proceeds to the American Cancer Society. This way, everyone who buys this book will also be helping those people who turn to the ACS during their time of need.

INTRODUCTION

Anne Mitchell lives in Evergreen, Colorado, with her husband and young daughter. Her career has been devoted to the field of graphic design. This is her first book.

———

I was a smoker for over 25 years. I smoked about a pack a day and maybe inhaled another pack when I went out drinking. I started smoking when I was

15 years old. I first tried to quit when I was 18.

About six years ago, a series of events occurred that finally forced me to face my growing problem with another addiction: alcohol. I also came to realize that I would never quit smoking if I didn't first stop drinking. And for a long time, I just wasn't ready to stop drinking, party girl that I thought I was. Alcoholic woman is what I had become. That was a difficult pill to swallow at first, but with the loving support of friends and family, I slowly came to terms with this reality. When the obsession to drink was finally lifted by the grace of God, I thought I would soon be ready to look at this other problem of mine.

Well, it turned out that quitting drinking was a walk in the park compared to quitting smoking. This is not meant to minimize the struggle I had with alcohol. I think that, by anyone's measure, I was a serious alcoholic. But, once I *admitted* that, the struggle was over. Not so with cigarettes. They had a hold on me that was frightening in its tenacity.

I made hundreds, maybe thousands of attempts to quit smoking in recent years. Sometimes these attempts lasted hours and sometimes they lasted as long as four or five months. My calendar was littered with quit dates. My body never knew from day to day if it was going to continue its tenuous recovery process or surrender to a fresh assault.

Becoming a mother a few years ago was a huge turning point in my life. I thought that surely *now* I would have the monumental inspiration needed to finally quit smoking for good. It didn't happen that way, although the guilt and self-recrimination really started to hit hard.

My desire to give my daughter the healthiest start possible in life was strong enough to keep me smoke-free during most of my pregnancy. I was also able to remain mostly smoke-free during the time I breastfed her. But not entirely.

Every time I broke down and had a cigarette, it only made my cravings more intense. The struggle to control my smoking was very difficult, and I just couldn't seem to stop for good.

I tried nicotine gum, the patch, nicotine inhalers, reading stop-smoking books, writing in a journal, detox teas, toothpicks and carrot sticks, exercise, reading self-help books, vegetarianism, counseling, starting a stop-smoking program at work, eating organic foods, meditation, yoga, lollipops, and Zyban.®

I tried prayer, aromatherapy, reading books on understanding addictions, marrying a non-smoker, working a 12-step program, quitting with a buddy, asking my baby daughter for strength, reading books on how women can finally quit smoking, surfing the Web for information, hypnotherapy, chocolate therapy, herbal tonics, the patch again, watching videos on how to quit, buying shorter cigarettes, and positive visualization.

I switched brands, bought a new car that I vowed never to smoke in (that idea lasted a few weeks anyway), juiced fresh fruits to drink every morning, wrote down all of the reasons I wanted to quit and carried that list with me everywhere, and even made bargains with God.

I tried vitamins, positive thinking, listening to the tapes that came with some of the books in my growing library, buying a pack of cigarettes and throwing most of it out (I went through lots of money using this approach), watching that movie about the sleaziness of the cigarette industry, and reading a few more books on how dangerous smoking was and how to finally quit for good.

I even watched my grandmother become reliant on an oxygen tank then waste away and die from emphysema, lung cancer, and colon cancer after a lifetime of smoking.

I slowly discovered that it would take more than fear, willpower, or healthy eating to overcome this incredible addiction to cigarettes. I was starting to believe I would never be able to quit for good. Yet I knew it was hurting me. I often felt short of breath. I even had trouble singing to my little girl without the frog in my throat making an appearance.

In my desperation, I turned to hypnotherapy once again. My hypnotherapist was gracious enough to tape the session for me, and as I listened to it night after night, I thought about how powerful the spoken word was.

What if I had something equally powerful to listen to while I was driving down the road? Something that would help to reinforce my decision to remain smoke-free? A recording that would give me pause at work if I had a bad day?

An inspiration arose out of my musings. What if I could get people to talk about their own struggles with smoking? Even talk about the terrible physical price they or their loved ones may have paid for their addictions to cigarettes?

I reflected back on all of the conversations about smoking that I had been involved in over the years. Recalled all of the friends who struggled repeatedly to quit; the teenagers who talked about quitting soon; and the stories of pain and suffering caused by cancer, emphysema, and other smoking-related illnesses. Maybe I could persuade some people to share their tales. And maybe they would inspire other people to quit smoking too.

Indeed, some caring individuals did come forward who were willing to talk. These folks all shared a common hope: that you would listen to their stories and be moved to finally stop smoking. That you would perhaps see your own future in their tales and wish for something different for yourself. That the seriousness of this matter would become real for you too, without you actually having to live through it.

As I listened to these stories being told, it became easy to see that they all had a similar in-your-face kind of reality that was impossible to ignore. Scenes like these were playing out for someone somewhere every single day, and I had been dancing around the issue for years as though I was somehow immune.

I finally knew in my heart that I had to quit smoking for good, and that I had to do it now. I could no longer view cigarettes as my refuge. Once I made the decision that this was what I had to do and I began to feel with a powerful inner certainty that I *could* do it, it happened. I was free. And I believe this book and CD will help you reach that point, too.

———

This book does not contain any magic formula that will make you quit. There are no steps to go through or pills to take.

What you have in these pages are reminders of what you are doing to yourself each time you light up and information on why it can be so difficult to quit and so easy to relapse.

What is most important about this book is that by reading it you will learn what it takes to quit smoking for good and hopefully be inspired to take this critical step toward a new, healthier life.

In order for you to be truly successful, you need to decide that you *must* quit, believe that you *can* quit, and really feel all of this in your heart. Listening to the *Give It Up!* CD will help you start really feeling it, not just thinking it.

Humans are very auditory creatures, and listening to reinforcing messages can be a powerful way to help alter our inner self-talk. Think about how music has almost no emotional meaning when you experience it as written notes on a page. It's when we hear it come to life that our hearts beat faster, and we are moved. In the same way, listening to these people talk about their experiences is much more potent than just reading their stories.

Listen whenever you feel vulnerable. Listen to reinforce your success. You will probably relate to several stories. Go back to those often. The people who are speaking are trying to reach you in the hopes that something positive will result. They want you to succeed. And you can. You will. Start listening now.

Together, we hope that you will be inspired to cut short how long cigarettes will continue to be a part of your life, instead of cutting short your life.

Part One

Beyond the
Smoke Screen

WHY YOU SMOKE

You have probably heard that smoking can have some devastating consequences. What you may not know is that at least one person is dying *every minute* in this country because they were smokers. Others are dying because they lived or worked with someone who smoked. Some of these secondary victims are children and some are unborn infants.

Not all of the adults who die of smoking are old either. Because more people are starting to smoke at a younger age, when lungs are still maturing, lung cancers are also appearing earlier.

The average age a smoker starts smoking is 13. Again, that's the *average* age. This means that

88 percent of adult smokers tried their first cigarette before age 18.

some may start when they are younger than 10 and others not until they're 16 or 17. We think of 13 as too young to drive, to vote, and perhaps even to date. So why are they smoking?

Well, for one thing, they see adults like us smoking. They want to appear "mature." They see beautiful, healthy models portrayed in cigarette advertising. They see major sporting events being sponsored by the cigarette industry. Their parents and teachers tell them not to, so it becomes a point of rebellion. They see friends and classmates smoke. They see smokers in movies and movie stars who smoke. They probably even have family members who smoke.

In the United States alone, over 3,000 children become new smokers *every day.* Think back to why and when you started. As a kid, did you ever wish for the day when you would be free to smoke wherever and as often as you liked and not have to sneak or hide? Did you look up to adults who smoked?

The younger you are when you start smoking, the more likely you are to become addicted and to be a heavy smoker later in life. You are also more likely to die prematurely than a smoker who starts smoking later in life.

Some kids may even begin smoking by telling themselves they'll only do it for a little while, maybe a year or two. Unfortunately, smoking is perceived by many young people as a choice one makes in a free world. The advertising industry fuels this notion by using models that appear healthy and attractive, even invincible to smoking's harms. These "happy smokers" supposedly express their individuality and love for life through their choice of cigarette brand.

There are even activist groups devoted to smoker's rights. The cigarette industry tells us it's a decision adults choose to make. They claim they are just filling a demand.

What they don't tell you is that once you start smoking, the choice factor rapidly disappears. You become compelled to smoke. Your brain becomes addicted very quickly. It's getting an immediate rush with very little effort expended. It wants more. Rationalization begins. After all, you're just smoking one cigarette at a time. How much can one cigarette hurt?

Well, a smoker doesn't stop at one cigarette, of course. A smoker makes sure that they have more for later. Makes sure there will be an opportunity to smoke later. Feels the craving for another cigarette not too long after having the last. May even, when under stress, quickly go through a whole pack.

Smokers smoke to feel calm, to perk up, to

concentrate, to relax, to celebrate, to commiserate, to talk on the phone, to drive to work, to socialize, to be left alone, to be creative, to kill time, to stave off hunger, to finish a meal, to enjoy coffee, to get through work, and just to be. In other words, smokers smoke whenever they feel they need to and for whatever reasons come up.

Smoking becomes such a large part of your life in part because, in order to feel normal, you need to ingest nicotine at a regular rate. You may even be addicted to some of the 4,000 other chemicals in cigarettes.

Many smokers either start out on or switch to light cigarettes, thinking that they are somehow helping themselves to avoid harm. People who smoke light cigarettes tend to inhale more deeply and hold it in longer. The reason for this is the need for the body's cells to attain and maintain a certain level of nicotine in order for the smoker to feel "right" again. A light cigarette gets in the way of that, so the smoker unconsciously compensates by taking deeper drags and taking longer to exhale. This more intense way of smoking may cause lung cancers to develop deeper in the lungs, which makes them both more difficult to detect and more challenging to treat.

Even the way commercial cigarettes are made may cause people to smoke more. Filters interfere with the amount of nicotine ingested, so smokers may dose themselves more intensely and more frequently to make up for that. Filters also block out the larger particulates that would have caused irritation, removing another reason for the smoker to moderate their intake.

7 people every minute throughout the world die from a tobacco-related illness (that's 4 million this year).

However, these filters still allow the smaller particulates in, and consequently, there has been an increase in certain types of lung cancer.

There are indications that nicotine and other chemicals have been added to heighten addiction and increase the smoker's pleasure. Few people can smoke less than a half a pack a day, needing to replenish their bodies regularly with their drug. The portability and accessibility of smoking materials has also helped to make it a worldwide epidemic.

It's possible that you're smoking because you want to. It's far more likely that you're smoking because you have to. Your brain feels threatened with the prospect of losing its drug, so it will give you lots of trouble if you try to stop.

It's your addicted brain we're talking about here, and it will come up with all kinds of rationalizations, deceptive thinking, excuses, and self-pity talks. It will feign ignorance and develop a really short memory. It will do everything it can to talk you back into supplying its drug of choice.

Your brain is a powerful instrument, yet nicotine has enslaved it. Nicotine is a very intense drug. In one study, volunteers were injected with doses of amphetamine, cocaine, and nicotine, and they could not tell the difference between the three.

You may have tried to quit before, maybe even many times before. If you were ever tempted to smoke after quitting, and did so by telling yourself "I'll only have one," it was very likely you didn't stop at just one. Just a tiny bit of nicotine whets your appetite and awakens that sleeping monster of craving. It is almost impossible to control the use of this drug by willpower alone.

But this is not about willpower or strength of character. It is about addiction. Addicts have trouble believing they can live without their drug. That's how addiction works. You smoke because you are a smoker, and you remain a smoker because you can't stop smoking. This may seem rather simplistic, but the point is that the cycle self-perpetuates. You have to do something pretty aggressive to break it.

Think about those people in your life who would be extremely grateful and relieved if you never smoked again. Then think about those who don't ever want to see you stop, at least not until you die.

Spending on tobacco advertising went from 6.73 billion dollars in 1998 to 8.24 billion dollars in 1999.

The tobacco industry certainly does not want to see you quit. They like having you as a role model for new smokers. They like the steady reliability of your money. The advertising industry does not want to see you quit either. They like the tobacco industry's money.

The magazine-publishing industry does not want to see you quit. Tobacco advertisers pay big bucks to place ads in their publications. Magazine editors may even hesitate to publish anti-smoking articles because the advertisers might pull their ads from what they believe is a nonsupportive venue. More on this topic can be found in Part Four's chapter *The target is you.*

There are lots of other businesses that would prefer that you remain a smoker. Think about producers of cigarette cases, matches, lighters, ashtrays, breath mints, and smoker's toothpastes. Some people even view the medical industry as a beneficiary. The list can go on and on.

75 percent of smokers say they want to quit.

There is probably a part of you that does not want to see yourself quit. Cigarettes are an old reliable friend, always there during troubled times and helping you celebrate the good times. How will you ever live without them? Of course the real question is what kind of a life are you doomed to live with them?

It's been documented that smokers are more likely to have fewer years of education or to be in a lower-income bracket. Perhaps it's coupled with a sense of hopelessness or futility. Are you one of those people? Do you wish for more out of your life? Have you thought about how smoking might be holding you back?

Our horizons become limited by this addiction and by the physical and social

Approximately 3 out of 4 people do not smoke.

consequences of feeding that addiction. Perhaps we seek a perverse kind of safety net or a way to avoid disappointment. This kind of logic says, "If I don't really try, I won't have to call it failure."

Do you find yourself planning and thinking about your next fix? Think about how many times you've let yourself run out of your drug. What lengths have you gone to for a smoke? How long will you let this thing continue to rule your life?

Do you find yourself obsessing about smoking, especially when you can't smoke? Do you get irritated with others if they stand in the way of you and your next cigarette? Do you use smoking to control your weight? Do you sometimes decide to smoke because "I just deserve it, damnit"? Do you find yourself feeling depressed or even crazy over your inability to stop?

When you're a smoker, you need nicotine just to feel normal. You may think cigarettes calm you down. In fact, smokers have been found to experience stress more acutely than nonsmokers, in part because nicotine *causes* physical stress.

When your nicotine level drops low, it becomes difficult to concentrate or relax until you can get replenished. Then you feel calm and back to normal. But your normal is not the same as a non-smoker's normal.

You may have consciously or unconsciously used cigarettes to avoid your feelings. When you first quit, you may feel kind of raw for a while. This can be expected since you have been clouding your thinking and your mind for so long. You have probably been stuffing your anger away and putting up a rather effective smoke screen to keep others at a distance. And if you haven't fully experienced your feelings, you possibly haven't gotten to know yourself very well either.

If, like most people, you started smoking as a teenager, your self-image is probably all tied up with smoking. You have an internal picture of yourself, and it may be hard to imagine that picture without cigarettes.

You know smoking hurts you, yet you continue to do it. It's unfortunate that the effects are invisible for so long. That helps in the self-deception. In fact, there's pretty much only one way for this to turn out if you remain a smoker. Despite hearing about smokers who have lived into their nineties, the fact is that most people are badly harmed by the effects of smoking. What's at stake here is not how long you might live, but what kind of life you will be left with if you manage to survive and grow old.

We say things like "I'll quit on my birthday"

50 percent of current smokers will die from a smoking-related illness.

or "I'm going to quit some-day, just not today." But you have to ask yourself why _not_ today? How many "not todays" are you planning on stringing together? Another year's worth? Another 10 years' worth?

You may have been the kind of smoker who would never leave home without their cigarettes. Think about how you would feel if you couldn't go anywhere without your oxygen tank.

Smoking harms us spiritually too. You may not be religious or even consider yourself spiritual. But there's no denying the fact that by smoking we are doing something that is anti-life. The conflict that this creates in us chips away at our feelings of self-worth, diminishing our self-respect. It may even perpetuate our self-destructiveness: "I smoke, therefore I am bad. I am bad, therefore I smoke."

Do you see cigarettes as your friend, helpful through thick and thin? Would you stay friends with someone who was trying to kill you?

HOW SMOKING HURTS YOU

It's been said that if the full damage caused by cigarettes was visible on the outside of the body, nobody would ever smoke. Let's start with what we *can* see.

If you are young, you may not be seeing any wrinkles yet. When you do start seeing them though, they will come faster and more abundantly than they will with your nonsmoking friends.

Smoking increases the presence of free radicals, which cause damage to your skin and elsewhere. Nicotine interferes with the functioning of your sweat glands, resulting in dry skin. Collagen actually changes its structure because of its constant exposure to the poisons in cigarettes. Blood vessels constrict, reducing the flow of nutrients to the skin. You are essentially cooking yourself, slowly getting smoked just like a sardine.

Smoking strips your body of essential vitamins like A and C. The B vitamins are also depleted. Because of this vitamin deficiency, your cells can't repair as quickly or efficiently. You don't recover from wounds or illnesses as easily as a nonsmoker. You can take vitamins to help offset some of these deficiencies, but keep in mind that smoking impedes the ability of your body to fully utilize them.

Recent findings suggest that heavy smokers who also have a diet high in polyunsaturated fats may be causing the vitamin E they ingest to function as a pro-oxidant instead of as an antioxidant. In other words, this normally beneficial vitamin can actually cause harm instead of protect.

Your hair also suffers. It becomes more dry and brittle over time. If a scientist closely studied a strand of your hair, she would see your smoking history in its cells.

Now, look in a mirror and open your mouth. A healthy tongue is pink and smooth, without indentations, grooves, or a coating on it. Smoking raises the temperature inside your mouth, causing cell damage and death. Your gums may be receding or reddened by the early effects of gum disease.

Your teeth are probably yellow. The chemical balance of your saliva is altered by smoking, as is the amount. This affects how well your mouth can keep itself clean, which can result in plaque buildup and cavities.

A dentist can look in your mouth and pretty

much see whether or not you're a smoker. It's not just the smell.

Look at the back of your throat. Is it healthy-looking? Have you thought about what it might feel like to be unable to swallow or even to breathe because of a tumor?

Smell your hands. Not just your fingertips, but your palms. Your body is constantly trying to excrete the poisons introduced by smoking. One of the ways it does this is through your sweat glands. Try smelling your hands first thing in the morning before your first cigarette. When you're continuously sweating toxins, your whole body takes on an unmistakable odor.

On any given day in the U.S., over 450 people will receive a diagnosis of lung cancer.

Now let's look at what's going on inside your body. Your blood pressure increases by 10–20 points almost immediately after taking a drag from a cigarette. Your heart beats faster. Your metabolism increases. Your higher metabolism is one way that your body tries to expel the ever-present toxic materials. It is similar to the way your body uses a fever to get rid of a virus.

Your heart beats more rapidly in its desperate attempt to supply your cells with oxygen-rich blood. Smoking causes reduced oxygen flow, which affects the health of every part of your body. Without plenty of life-giving and cleansing oxygen, your body cannot thrive. Cells mutate and die. Some cells mutate and don't die. They begin to multiply and become cancerous.

Carbon monoxide molecules bind much more readily to red blood cells than do oxygen molecules. This reduces the oxygen level in your blood, causing you to feel drained and tired.

One of the reasons smoking feels so good so fast is because we inhale the drug into our lungs, which brings it directly into our bloodstream. We get our drug within seconds.

Of course this means that everything else that comes along for the ride is also going straight into your lungs and bloodstream. Your blood carries this stuff very efficiently to every part of you.

Every cell in your body is exposed to the mutagens and carcinogens in cigarettes. Every cell in your nails, your blood vessels, your heart, your brain, your eyes, and your sex organs is affected. There are over 4,000 chemicals in cigarettes, 43 of which are known to cause cancer. Not suspected of causing cancer, *known* to cause it. And by smoking, you actually reduce the ability of your body to withstand this onslaught.

In 1994, tobacco companies listed 599 ingredients they routinely added to cigarettes. This disclosure was in response to a U.S. Food and Drug Administration directive.

When you swallow and your saliva is filled

with the by-products of smoking, it's not too difficult to imagine those by-products permeating your whole digestive system, leaving a trail of poisons behind to work their damage.

One of smoking's by-products is tar. This material builds up on the inside of your body, kind of like the way sludge can build up inside your bathroom sink drainpipe. Over time, your lungs and even your heart can become discolored and damaged by black tar.

Smoking leaches calcium from your system. It also reduces levels of estrogen, a hormone that helps bones hang onto calcium and other bone-strengthening minerals. Osteoporosis and an increased risk of hip fracture can result.

Estrogen helps women keep their feminine waistlines. Apple-shaped figures (bodies with a high waist-to-hip ratio) are common among smokers and are also associated with heart problems.

Reduced estrogen levels can cause menopause to come early, bringing increased risk of heart disease. Some smokers may experience more severe menopausal symptoms.

Smoking can interfere with fertility by damaging eggs and reducing sperm count. It can also cause impotence, delayed conception, birth defects, and miscarriage.

Smoking releases hormones that inhibit wound healing. Smokers don't recover from surgery nearly as quickly as nonsmokers. Smokers can anticipate longer hospital stays, more medication, and an increased risk of infection.

Smoking reduces blood flow to the brain. You may think it helps you to concentrate and that you feel foggy when you try to quit, but this is because your brain got used to its drug and to its oxygen-starved condition. When you quit, you are suddenly allowing your brain to receive normal levels of oxygen (no wonder you may feel like an airhead at times when you first quit).

Your body is more vulnerable to environmental toxins. If a smoker and a nonsmoker are both exposed to similar levels of pollutants or toxic chemicals for equal amounts of time, the smoker stands a greater chance of being adversely affected since their immune system has been compromised.

If you smoke around children, please keep these facts in mind. Children exposed to secondary smoke have a higher incidence of

Almost half of the world's children breathe second-hand smoke.

impaired lung development. They suffer more allergies and respiratory diseases, like bronchitis and pneumonia, and have ear infections more frequently. They have an increased risk of gastrointestinal disease. They can be slower in developing reading, math, and spelling skills. They also tend to be more hyperactive, to have shorter attention spans, and to develop behavioral problems.

And when kids grow up seeing a parent or other family member smoke, they are far more likely to become smokers themselves.

Teenagers who smoke affect the growth and maturation of their lungs. Lungs don't stop developing until people are well into adulthood. A smoker who starts at age 13 will have caused measurable physical damage by the time they are fully grown.

Pregnant women who smoke have increased risks of stillbirth, premature delivery, and having low-birth-weight babies. Infants of smokers are at a higher risk of becoming victims of Sudden Infant Death Syndrome (SIDS).

The total annual economic burden of cigarette smoking in the U.S. may exceed 135 billion dollars.

Take a look at the following list of smoking-related ailments. They range from the irritating and uncomfortable to the debilitating and deadly. This list is not necessarily complete. If you want more information, please refer to the recommended reading list and Web sites noted in the back of this book.

Smoking is a direct cause of or is implicated as a risk factor in the following illnesses and conditions:

- bad breath
- brain cancer
- burns
- cancer of the digestive organs

  (anal, colon, stomach)
- cancer of the genital and urinary area

  (bladder, cervical, kidney, pancreatic,

  penile, prostate, vulvar)
- cancer of the head and neck

  (esophagus, larynx, lip, mouth, nasal,

  pharynx, salivary gland, sinus, tongue)
- cancer of the lymphatic system
- cataracts

- cerebrovascular disease

- chronic bronchitis

- cough

- damaged blood vessels

- depression

- diminished sense of smell and taste

- ear infections

- early menopause (which results in
  a higher risk of both osteoporosis and
  heart disease)

- emphysema

- eye disease, resulting in sudden vision
  loss (anterior ischemic optic neuropathy)

- fetal and neonatal death

- gingivitis

- headaches

- hearing loss

- heart disease

- high blood pressure

- immunological deficiencies

- impotence

- incontinence

- infertility

- insulin resistance, resulting in

  diabetes mellitus

- leukemia

- low energy

- lung cancer

- miscarriage

- osteoporosis

- peptic ulcer disease

- periodontal disease

- pneumonia and influenza

- poor circulation

- premature wrinkling

- psoriasis

- racing heart

- shortness of breath

- sinusitis

- snoring

- stroke

- yellow teeth

For the complete horror story, read *Cigarettes: What The Warning Label Doesn't Tell You*, by Dr. Elizabeth Whelan and the American Council on Science and Health.

Many people buy lottery tickets thinking they have a chance of winning big money, even though the odds are worse than a million-to-one.

90 percent of lung cancer deaths are attributed to smoking.

Yet they think it's the other guy who will get lung cancer when the odds are more than 1 in 5. At least we can say optimism is alive and well.

The next time you lay down money for cigarettes, think about what the real price is. You're paying for your life force to go up in smoke and for your vital energy to be drained. You may even be paying with your life itself.

The equivalent of several jumbo jets full of people dies *each day* in this country of smoking-related illnesses. Are you buying a ticket on one of those planes?

Part Two

Gaining Clarity

THE BENEFITS OF QUITTING

Much of the damage caused by smoking is reversible, but you have to quit smoking to start experiencing recovery. People who quit smoking live longer, healthier lives on average than those who continue to smoke.

When you first quit smoking, you may find yourself having to clear your throat more often and coughing up mucus. Smoking kills off cilia that, when healthy, help keep your air passages clean.

Increased mucus production in the lungs is a protective reaction to the presence of dead cilia. Once you quit, your body works on ridding itself of this excess mucus and debris.

Soon after you quit, you may feel tingling in your limbs or extremities. This is caused by your circulation returning to normal. You may find headaches disappearing. You will begin to feel more energetic as your body receives more oxygen.

You will notice the smells of fresh air, flowers, grass, and of that person smoking yards away. You will probably start choosing healthier foods, since your body will crave what's good for it. Meals will taste better.

You will find yourself developing an aversion to the smell of smoke and wishing for clean air wherever you go. You will feel sorry for smokers who are still tied to their deadly habit.

You will feel clean, powerful, and intelligent

as you begin to reap the rewards of becoming a nonsmoker. You are doing what you know to be right. It feels really good to be good to yourself. You will never want to go back to that other place again.

The following information comes from the American Cancer Society and outlines some of the benefits of becoming an ex-smoker:

20 minutes after quitting smoking
- blood pressure drops to a level close to
  that before the last cigarette
- temperature of hands and feet
  increases to normal

8 hours after quitting smoking
- carbon monoxide level in blood
  drops to normal

24 hours after quitting smoking
- chance of heart attack decreases

2 weeks to 3 months after quitting smoking

- circulation improves

- lung function increases up to 30 percent

1–9 months after quitting smoking

- coughing, sinus congestion, fatigue,

  shortness of breath decrease

- cilia regain normal function in lungs,

  increasing ability to handle mucus,

  clean the lungs, reduce infection

1 year after quitting smoking

- excess risk of coronary heart disease

  is half that of a smoker's

5–15 years after quitting smoking

- stroke risk is reduced to that of a

  nonsmoker's

10 years after quitting smoking

- lung cancer death rate about half that

  of a continuing smoker's

- risk of cancer of the mouth, throat,

  esophagus, bladder, kidney, and

  pancreas decreases

15 years after quitting smoking

- risk of coronary heart disease is that

  of a nonsmoker's

As you can see, some benefits are immediate and some take much longer. But you have to start somewhere, and it all happens one day at a time.

A VISION FOR YOU

If you have tried to quit time and time again without any lasting success, you may have begun to feel that this whole business of quitting is rather futile. Riding the fence can be exhausting, jumping back and forth, unsure of which side you want to stay on. This ambivalence is quite common for smokers.

When you say to yourself "I want to quit smoking" or "I know I should quit," and yet you continue to smoke, think about which part of you wants to quit and which part of you is not yet ready.

Let's call the part of you that wants to quit your

"higher self." And the part of you that wants to

88 percent of successful ex-smokers quit cold turkey.

continue its self-destructive, addictive behavior we'll call your "ego."

Your higher self intuitively knows what is good for you. You were born with the capacity to tap into this self-wisdom. That little voice that keeps telling you to quit smoking is coming from this center of self-knowledge and self-interest. When you are in harmony with the needs of your higher self, you are filled with peace and serenity.

Deciding to quit is an act of surrender. You are surrendering to the demands of your higher self. Your higher self has never stopped wishing goodness and health for you. It has been patiently waiting for the rest of you to want that too.

You become what you listen to and what you

think about. When your internal self-talk is filled with positive messages of desires for health and well-being, you become that. It enters your sub-conscious. The more you think it, the more it becomes you.

Your ego will do everything that it can to get in the way of this process. Your ego is driven by your brain, which doesn't always have your best interests in mind when it's making choices for you. Remember that your brain is very susceptible to addiction. Addicted behavior is not rational behavior. Part of you may still want to smoke, but you're not going to let that part make the day-to-day decisions anymore.

Do you find yourself saying, "Someday I'll quit, I'm just not ready right now" or "I've got too much going on in my life right now to stop smoking"? That was your ego telling you that it wants its drug just a little bit longer. It does not want you to stop smoking, at least not today.

It seems rather odd if you stop and think about it. Your ego goes to such lengths to get its way and yet, at the same time, seems utterly unaware that the eventual result of its actions is to self-destruct.

You do not have to fight this battle any longer. You do not have to procrastinate. Your life does not have to be flawless, with the planets in perfect alignment, for you to take this step. You might hear others talk about how hard it is to quit, and you start to believe it for yourself. But you don't have to buy into that. You can begin your life of freedom now. The life you were meant to live. The life your higher self needs for you to live.

Once you have removed the cloud that was your addiction, you will begin to have clarity about what you need to do. You will reach the point where smoking is no longer an option. You know it's been slow suicide. You know that even if you don't die from cancer, you will likely suffer and die from some other smoking-related illness. You know there can be very serious conse-quences if you continue to smoke. You know you cause harm to others if you smoke around them.

8 nonsmokers will die of lung cancer today because they were exposed to second-hand smoke.

There is another force interested in seeing your higher self reach its potential. We could call that force God, or Goddess, or Nature. If the word God makes you uncomfortable, try using another word. All the word does is represent something out there that is not you but that is responsible for you and for everything you see.

On the next page is a prayer or saying that may be helpful for you. Say it whenever you feel your ego trying to take over.

———

God, grant me the serenity

to accept the things I cannot change,

the courage to change the things I can,

and the wisdom to know the difference.

attributed to Friedrich Oetinger

———

You will find the courage to stop. It's already waiting inside of you. You only need to believe in it to tap into it.

You come to see what you believe in. If you believe the world is a friendly place where people are basically good, then that is what you will encounter in your daily interactions. If you believe people are selfish creatures who are hostile and only out for themselves, then that is probably what you will encounter. If you believe you have the power within you to make a change as life-altering as this, then you will find it within yourself to do so. If you believe you are captive to the power of cigarettes, then that is how you will remain.

If you believe there is an ultimate authority out there and within you that is deeply interested in seeing you succeed, then you will have access to that power. There are loving and benevolent influences all around you waiting to help. Call them your angels or spirit guides, gods or forces, or even your friends and family. Your higher self has been waiting for the day when you would choose to rise above your ego and fulfill your destiny of health and freedom. You are not alone.

With your newfound freedom, you will stand tall and proud, knowing that you are in harmony with your universe. You will come to have higher self-esteem. You may have thought that good self-esteem was needed first in order for you to be able to do something brave or new. In fact, improved self-esteem is one of the positive results of doing something brave and new.

Imagine yourself addiction-free. You will have more energy and more time. Think of how much time was spent on smoking, preparing to smoke, and cleaning up from smoking. What will you do with this time now? Will you use it to be creative, read, or play more with your child or pet? Will you use it to exercise, meditate, or even pick up a new hobby? Your choices are endless, and your world just got a little bigger.

Making healthy choices makes you feel physically whole and emotionally and spiritually complete. You will not sense that emptiness that you used to try to fill with cigarette smoke. You have a heightened sense of well-being. You breathe deeply of the life-giving air around you.

Think about your breathing for a moment. Notice if only your upper chest moves as you breathe. This is shallow breathing. It does not pull oxygen deep into your lungs to be fully exchanged with the old carbon dioxide.

Now take a deep breath, trying to pull the air into your stomach. Women in particular tend not to breathe this way because it can make their tummies stick out. But shallow breathing robs you of vital air. Your body is left in a constant state of need. You are worth as much oxygen as your body can take in so that it feels completely saturated and nourished.

You may need to practice full breathing for some time before it becomes second nature. Do it consciously whenever you can. It is a great way to calm yourself and to get centered.

As you breathe, visualize your lungs, heart, and esophagus. Feel those pink, spongy, healthy lungs taking in life-giving oxygen. Imagine those oxygen molecules traveling freely throughout your body and into your arms, hands, and fingers; your legs, feet, and toes; your brain, eyes, and lips.

Now imagine breathing in a mouthful of smoke. Your lungs, heart, and brain eagerly anticipate oxygen but get carbon monoxide, nicotine, and other poisons instead. They get cheated and starved. They accept in silence, for now.

Now, relax as you breathe deeply of clean air instead. Roll your shoulders. Loosen your jaw. Wiggle your toes. You are becoming less tense and more laid back. Little things don't bother you as easily. You have more patience.

What follows are some life-affirming messages for you to absorb as you move toward your new life of liberation from addiction.

- I crave freedom and a healthy life.

- Physical activity feels great. I can feel
  my lungs working better.

- I feel bathed in a glow of optimism.
  I can now let go of my addiction.

- I want a fresh glass of cold water to
  hydrate and cleanse my body.

- I want juice and fruit and vegetables.

- I have decided that these things are more
  important to me than cigarettes.

- I am not helpless in the face of my
  addiction to cigarettes.

• I choose to surrender to the power of
  my higher self, instead of to nicotine.

• I choose not to smoke. I choose life.

• I am worthy of success. I will succeed.

Your newfound clarity will see you through any temptations. Friends who still suffer from an addiction to smoking will see the change in you and be inspired. You will become a very special kind of role model. You are developing your new identity as a vigorous person who loves life and makes smart choices for optimal health.

You came into this world smoke-free. You will be smoke-free again. You are a nonsmoker by nature, you know.

Part Three

Give It Up!

STOP SMOKING FOR LIFE

By now, you have probably come to see how you really weren't ever in control of your smoking. It was in control of you. You can finally surrender to the notion that you are powerless over your addiction. Give it up! Turn it over to God or to your higher self. You cannot "manage" this addiction. All you can do is give it up.

You are powerless over your cravings. You are not powerless over what you do about those cravings. If you get distracted by a craving, remember that it will go away within minutes. Eventually, the cravings will stop bothering you altogether. But they will never stop coming back if you keep feeding them by giving in and smoking.

A craving is like a wild animal. You feed it because at first it seems rather harmless. Soon it becomes a friend. Then one day it turns on you and causes you harm. That is only its nature.

Almost half of all people who have ever smoked have quit smoking.

You need to always remember that you are an addict, and that your addiction will be reactivated by contact with the drug.

Your cravings will leave you for good if you are patient and don't give in.

—

Statistics show that most successful ex-smokers quit cold turkey. However, you may decide that the patch, nicotine gum, or some other product will be helpful for you. This book and its companion CD can help you to be successful on your own, but you should do whatever feels right. Many people have successfully quit, using these methods.

Having a support group can also be a very important component of a successful smoking-cessation program. There are lots of good options out there, and it is recommended that you seriously consider them.

Recent studies have shown that people who smoke their first cigarette later in the morning and smoke fewer cigarettes per day are more likely to be successful in quitting smoking. How soon you smoke after waking and how often you smoke throughout the day are both indicators of your level of nicotine addiction. Those who are less addicted are more likely to be able to quit. If you are heavily addicted, you may need to cut back first in order to achieve long-term success.

———

Here are some tips to help you make *this* stop-smoking attempt your last.

• In the beginning, you will want to watch your intake of mood-altering substances like alcohol, caffeine, chocolate, and sugar.

• You should be careful not to indulge in lots of fatty foods or red meat. You will want to nurture your body and help it to run as cleanly and efficiently as possible as it recovers in the coming weeks and months.

• You may choose to investigate the use of herbs or nicotine-replacement therapies to help you deal with withdrawal symptoms. Consult first with your physician about possible drug interactions if you are taking other medications.

- Go to the dentist and have your teeth cleaned. You will enjoy the fresh feeling in your mouth, and you will remove built-up plaque and discoloration.

- Give your body plenty of whole grains, fruits, and vegetables. Snack on protein-packed seeds and nuts.

- Drink plenty of water. Add lemon, lime, or cucumber slices to the water to help cleanse your system and refresh yourself.

- Get some exercise every day, even if it's only by parking a little farther away so that you have to walk. Take the stairs instead of the elevator. You are detoxifying and reclaiming your energy. Let this energy work for you. You will be rewarded with a steady stream of endorphins, relaxing you and boosting your mood.

• Be careful if you are embarking on a new exercise program right as you quit smoking. This can be a valuable way to stay motivated, but if you are unable to stay with your new exercise routine because of illness, travel, or increased work demands, it might turn into an excuse to start smoking again. You might figure that if you can't be totally healthy, then you might as well smoke. Or the added stress might make you feel sorry for yourself. This note of caution is not intended to discourage you from exercise but to make you aware of possible pitfalls.

• Let the bad stuff just roll off your back. Remember that you can choose what your responses will be to the negative things in your life. You have that power.

• You may find yourself inspired to do other healthy things like floss more regularly or go on a diet. Just be careful not to try to remake yourself overnight. You don't need additional stress right now. Be gentle with yourself. It's okay to go slow and just tackle one thing at a time.

- Tell yourself, "Today I am free. I do not have to smoke. I am whole and complete just the way I am." Sunshine, breezes, and the smell of fresh rain will make you smile and will remind you of how nice it is not to smoke anymore.

- If you are used to weighing yourself frequently, give yourself a break and stop doing that. You can rely on how your clothes fit to tell you if you've had a weight change. Watching the dial on the scale every day will only drive you nuts and may even interfere with your resolve.

- Surround yourself with favorite scents. This will increase your awareness of your improving ability to smell. The essences of flowers, mint, or fresh fruit will remind you of how nice it is not to be living in that cloud of smoke. No more bad breath or stinky clothes, fingers, and hair. People will no longer smell that aura of smokiness when you enter a room.

• When you feel stressed, count slowly to 10, breathing in deeply and holding your breath like you would hold in a hit off a cigarette. Then think about how you are letting those oxygen molecules circulate freely throughout your body, unhampered by any smoke particles.

• Think now about how you will respond in a crisis, how you will choose *not* to return to cigarettes. Remember, if you smoke, it will not make the crisis go away, it will just make you a smoker again. Have a plan ready. Keep this book and the *Give It Up!* CD handy.

• If you feel a really intense craving, it may just be thirst. Your body might be trying to tell you it needs to be replenished, giving you that "empty, in need" feeling that you might mistake for withdrawal pangs. You are still learning to listen to your body. This may take some time, since you have ignored its needs for so long. Take a big drink of water, and see if you don't feel better.

• Give yourself small gifts with the money you're saving by not smoking. Go see a movie or get a massage. You deserve to spoil yourself a little.

• If you have a relapse, just remember it is not the end. It is a mistake. Treat it like one, and see what you can learn from it. What triggered you to relapse and how can you avoid that in the future? How can you change your response? And don't forget all of the good you just did for your body during the period when you didn't smoke. Your body wants more of that healing. Consider it practice. Your higher self wants you back on track. Your gratitude

The five-year survival rate for lung cancer is about 13 percent. This means 87 percent of those diagnosed with lung cancer will die within five years, some within weeks.

about your improving health will continue to grow until it is more powerful than any fleeting desire you might have to smoke.

It's time to put down this burden you've carried for so long and walk a little lighter. You don't have to hurt yourself anymore. You are a survivor.

THE STORIES

Quitting smoking is not usually the result of a rational decision. You can talk yourself out of it pretty easily if all you use is logic. It has to be an emotional decision, one that you feel in the very core of your being. You must create a new belief system around smoking. These new beliefs must be powerful enough to sustain you in times of stress and to motivate you in times of insecurity and doubt. The stories you will hear on the CD will help you develop this new belief system, reaching that part of you that needs to be reminded of how important this decision is. Listening will help drive these messages deeper into your conscious and subconscious thinking, touching you on an emotional and more elemental level. Once this new way of thinking is internalized, you cannot be swayed. You will have finally turned the corner.

The speakers are from all walks of life. Some of them are teens who are certain they will not smoke as adults. Others are adults who have struggled to quit many times over the years. And then there are the ones who speak of their own or a loved one's illness that was a result of smoking. Their messages are perhaps the most powerful of all. They each agreed to contribute because they wanted to help other people quit smoking. They are hoping you won't have to go through what they did, that you will stop in time.

Return to the stories that resonate for you. Listen as often as you need to. Every time that you think about wanting to smoke, you should listen to this recording. Listen while you drive and while you exercise. Listen as you fall asleep at night. Whenever you can, give yourself the opportunity to let these messages sink in.

You do not have to concentrate on the words; it is okay to let your mind wander as you listen. You can choose to listen only once, but keep in mind that the more you listen, the more deeply ingrained the verbal images will become.

The words you will hear are going to be both subtle and powerful, nudging you to where you want to go and empowering you to get there. Every time you hear the speakers, their words will become more hard-wired into your thinking. Soon, you will find phrases popping into your mind during your daily activities.

The next time you're thinking of lighting up a cigarette, remember these stories. You may choose to have a drink of water, go for a walk, or just take some deep breaths instead.

You might even wish to create your own recording. You can write and record a positive, life-affirming message for yourself using phrases that you may have read in this book, heard on the CD, or picked up elsewhere. If you have children, you might ask them to record a message for you that will help you to stay on track. Auditory messages can be extremely powerful. Your own voice and the voices of loved ones are perhaps the most powerful of all. Whatever will work is what you should do. This is truly a matter of life and death.

Your new, healthier life is not on hold anymore. Push the Play button, and give yourself a fresh beginning.

THE SPEAKERS

What follows is a little information about the people who speak on the CD.

Jen is a new mother. She used to smoke heavily in college but wanted a healthier life for herself and her young family. She quit smoking a few years ago. She hopes being a part of this project will help keep her on track. She also hopes her message will be an inspiration to others who are struggling.

Greg quit smoking years ago after a bad case

of bronchitis. Now his father is dying of lung cancer. Several of his siblings still smoke. He hopes his father doesn't suffer too much. He wishes the rest of his family would stop smoking soon, before it's too late, but the topic is a difficult one to bring up.

Terri was told that she had a tumor on her vena cava and stopped smoking that very day. She underwent radiation and chemotherapy and is currently in remission. She prays that she will stay healthy and that the cancer won't return.

Joe watched his father die from lung cancer and was certain he would quit smoking soon after. Over a year later, he is still struggling with quitting. His mother also smokes heavily as do a couple of his siblings. He thought watching his father go through what he did would be enough to make them all want to quit, but so far it hasn't been. He hopes his contribution to the recording will not only help others, but himself and his family too.

Courtney and Robyn are sixteen-year-old twin sisters who recently quit smoking. They only smoked when they drank or hung out with friends. They don't ever want to become addicted, but aren't quite ready to say that they will never try it again.

Roxie has struggled to quit smoking for years, with intermittent periods of success. She is now watching her teen daughters (Courtney and Robyn) experiment with cigarettes. She hopes they don't follow her path but knows smoking can be a slippery slope.

Denise recently lost her father to lung cancer. She quit smoking soon after her father's diagnosis. Her father smoked for many years and died at the age of 54, only seven months after he was told he had cancer. Her mother also smokes. Denise hopes she won't have to watch her mother go through what her father went through.

Part Four

Woman to Woman

RECENT FINDINGS

There are certain things about smoking that affect women in particular. Increased risks related to pregnancy and childbirth and how smoking affects hormone levels and menopause are some of the special health issues female smokers face.

Women's concerns about various topics, such as empowerment and weight control, may also make them more vulnerable to cigarette advertising and other media influences related to smoking.

The Surgeon General of the United States recently released his report called *Women and Smoking*. The last time a report like this was issued was back in 1980. We've learned a lot in that time about the effects of smoking on women and about the roles that media and advertising have played.

Since 1980, approximately 3 million women have died prematurely because they smoked. Lung cancer was once rare for women, accounting for less than 5 percent of the deaths among women in 1930. It surpassed breast cancer in 1987.

An average of 14 years of life is lost for every woman who dies from smoking.

Lung cancer now accounts for 25 percent of all cancer deaths among U.S. women, and 90 percent of lung cancers are caused by smoking. The Surgeon General is calling this "a full-blown epidemic." This section is devoted to the topic of female smokers and the special concerns they face.

TOMORROW'S VICTIMS

Smoking prevalence among girls (and boys) was in decline starting in the 1970s. Then it began increasing again in the late 1990s. In 2000, 29.7 percent of high school senior girls and 32.8 percent of senior boys reported smoking in the last 30 days. In comparison, smoking prevalence is 22 percent among adult women and 26.4 percent among adult men.

We need to ask ourselves why so many of our young people are finding smoking desirable.

With everything we know, it seems like it ought to be going the other direction.

Whether someone becomes a smoker or not appears to be closely tied to their level of education. Among women with 9 to 11 years of schooling, approximately 33 percent are smokers; whereas, among women with 16 or more years of schooling, only 10 percent are smokers.

Some other predictors that a girl is likely to become a smoker are if she:

- has a parent who smokes

- has low self-esteem

- spends 10 or more hours per week
  at home without an adult present

- feels religion is not important

- has a best friend who smokes

- has below-average academic performance

- does not plan to complete college

- has a boyfriend who smokes

– diets or worries about her weight

– has a mother who smoked during

pregnancy

– has a sibling who smokes

– is not physically active

– has a poor father-daughter relationship

– suffers from depression

– perceives smoking to be a social "norm"

If a teenager has plenty of spending money, that teenager is more likely to smoke. This could be related to the fact that those who perform well in school are less likely to have jobs. Or it could simply be that those who work can better afford the habit.

A 1998 survey found that almost 65 percent of high school seniors prefer to date someone who doesn't smoke.

Teenage girls who smoke are far more likely to use alcohol, marijuana, and other drugs. Up to 77 percent of girls who smoke have used alcohol, and almost 50 percent engage in binge drinking or use marijuana.

Compare that to girls who have never smoked: 18 percent have used alcohol, 6 percent have engaged in binge drinking, and 3 percent have used marijuana. Binge drinking is defined here as consuming 5 or more drinks in a row.

Because smoking often precedes these other behaviors, it can be considered a "gateway" drug. Imagine what other problems we might prevent if we could just curb the number of children who start smoking.

———

The author conducted a focus group with six teenage girls who either smoked regularly or had experimented with smoking. Information was gathered about their smoking histories, preferences, and opinions on tobacco use. This was a very small group, and there was nothing scientific about the questions or the way in which the answers were gathered; however, it was still felt that there were some valuable observations to be shared.

One interesting finding was that none of these girls smoked so-called "feminine" cigarettes. In fact, they all smoked Marlboro Lights, believing the light brand was potentially less harmful than the full-strength brand. It was also perceived to be a smoother-tasting cigarette. They said that one reason they chose Marlboro was so they would be considered more down-to-earth girls, not putting on any airs. Another reason was that it was much easier to bum cigarettes from each other if everyone smoked the same brand. Most of the male smokers they know smoke Marlboro "reds," the regular-strength brand.

The three most heavily advertised cigarette brands are also the three top-selling brands. These are Marlboro, Camel, and Newport.

The girls all say it's very easy to obtain cigarettes from friends or at parties. Most friends have
an older sibling or boyfriend who will buy them
cigarettes. And everyone shares with everyone else.

Most of these young women consider themselves to be "binge" smokers, only smoking while
drinking at parties or when they are with friends. As
"social" smokers they have a hard time understanding why anyone would want to smoke when alone.

The few who smoke more regularly are
already trying to quit. They recognize the seeds of
addiction within themselves and suspect it might
be somewhat difficult to quit for good. None of
these girls see themselves as smokers a few years
from now. It is not something they want to be doing
in their twenties. They believe smoking is frowned
upon by many people.

They all remember being opponents of
smoking not so long ago, with some even being

involved in anti-smoking campaigns as middle-schoolers. They mentioned that there doesn't seem to be much anti-smoking activity targeted to kids in their age group, and that if there were, it might have helped them not to start (maybe).

On the other hand, they see smoking as a way to rebel against their parents, to explore new things, and to socialize and make new friends. In some ways they felt their child views on smoking were programmed into them, and once they experienced smoking for themselves, it wasn't as bad as they had been led to believe.

Children and teens who try to quit report the same withdrawal symptoms as adults and have the same problems with relapse.

Several girls recognized a negative physical effect after smoking just one cigarette, noticing how it affected their performance in sports and commenting on how they felt "icky" the next day. They said they never smoked before a big game.

Getting seriously ill from smoking seems very removed to these young women. They claim they will never allow themselves to get so addicted that they can't quit when they want to. They know it's harmful but don't believe they will be in harm's way, since this is such a temporary thing for them.

When these young women were asked if they knew that they were playing with fire, they all just kind of shrugged and smiled.

———

In one survey, 52.7 percent of female smokers aged 12 through 18 years did not expect to be smokers one year later. Of adult smokers surveyed, 44 percent believed they would not be smokers in five years. When followed up with five years later, 73 percent of these people were still smokers.

There is an epidemic going on, and these young women are at the center of it. They are making choices today that will affect them for the rest of their lives. These kids must be better armed with *all* of the facts so that they can make fully informed decisions and truly understand the risks and consequences of becoming a teenager who smokes.

COULD BE HAZARDOUS

Breasts, blood, and bearing babies are part of what defines womanhood. Raging hormones and hot flashes are part of what makes becoming an older woman so interesting. These physical characteristics are also part of why smoking can be so treacherous to a woman's health.

In addition to an increased risk for cancer, cardiovascular disease, and various respiratory illnesses, women who smoke are more susceptible to other health consequences. Some of them include:

- ectopic pregnancy

- hip fracture

- miscarriage

- more severe menopausal symptoms

- painful menstruation

- peptic ulcer

- premature delivery

- reduced bone density

- rheumatoid arthritis

Depression, bulimia, anxiety disorders, schizophrenia, attention deficit disorder, and alcoholism rates are also higher among smokers. The reasons for this are presently unknown. It could be that women who are more prone to these disorders are also more likely to become smokers. It may be a self-medicating response. Or there may even be an underlying cause-and-effect relationship.

———

Having a child is usually a time of joy and anticipation. But if the woman is a smoker, she will now be forced to deal with her nicotine addiction in addition to all of the physical changes that pregnancy brings. She is sure to know that smoking is not healthy for her or her baby. But what if she simply can't find a way to quit?

It is estimated that somewhere between 12 and 22 percent of pregnant women smoke during their pregnancy. But fortunately, smoking among pregnant women has been declining in recent years. Increased awareness of the harm smoking causes to an unborn child is certainly a key factor, but some of this reduction may be because pregnant smokers are less likely to report that they smoke because of the stigma attached to it.

The proportion of pregnant smokers who

smoke heavily is also in apparent decline; however, the total number of pregnant smokers is still

About one-third of women who quit smoking during pregnancy are still abstinent one year after giving birth.

devastatingly high, even though smoking during pregnancy is widely known to cause health complications and sometimes life-threatening conditions.

Smoking increases the risk of developing disorders that can lead to hemorrhaging and death for both mother and baby, such as premature rupturing of the membranes, abruptio placentae, and placenta previa. Pregnant smokers are also less likely to carry their babies to full term.

Ectopic pregnancy is the leading cause of maternal death in the first trimester and occurs more often among smokers than among nonsmokers.

Miscarriages among smokers appear to be dose-related, with heavier smokers being more likely to suffer miscarriage.

Stillbirths are another risk factor found to be increased among smokers.

Many chemicals in cigarettes are toxic or even deadly for the fetus, including nicotine and carbon monoxide. Getting enough oxygen and nutrients is more difficult for the baby in this polluted environment. One consequence can be low birth weight, which carries health risks ranging from neurosensory disabilities to cognitive and developmental delays. There can also be an increased risk of Sudden Infant Death Syndrome (SIDS).

There is evidence that the smoking status of the father also plays an important role in the health of the baby. Since the sperm supplies 50 percent of the child's genetic material, it makes sense that there might be problems if the man smokes.

When a pregnant woman lives with a smoker, her exposure to second-hand smoke can pose a serious health risk for both her and her baby. Low birth weight and fetal death are only two of many possible negative outcomes.

There are also limited studies showing a relationship between maternal and paternal smoking and increased rates of some congenital malformations, including cleft palate and urogenital or gastrointestinal defects.

Hopefully, education will continue to make a difference in how many women choose not to expose their unborn children to these risks.

There is one final encouraging note: Women are more likely to quit smoking during pregnancy than at any other time in their lives.

THE TARGET IS YOU

Women make the majority of purchasing decisions in this country. Many studies have been done to better understand what influences a woman to choose a certain product. Women also purchase most of the books and magazines that are published.

The tobacco industry must reach its target market with its advertising campaigns and promotions in order to increase sales, so it will go where the traffic is.

Many publications rely on cigarette advertising for a percentage of their revenue. This has been shown to have a direct impact on how likely these publications are to run reports on the hazards of tobacco use.

Twelve popular women's magazines were found to run 536 health-related articles during a

The World Health Organization predicts that if smoking prevalence continues to increase at the current rate, the annual number of tobacco-related deaths will reach 10 million by 2030.

twelve-year period. Only 24 articles about smoking ran in those magazines during this same twelve-year period. Eleven of those articles ran in *Good Housekeeping*, which does not accept cigarette advertising. This means the other eleven magazines ran an average of one article *per decade* that helped inform their readers about smoking's harms.

One study of five women's magazines that accepted cigarette advertising found only eight newsbriefs focused on smoking and health over a five-year period. None of these briefs mentioned lung cancer, heart disease, or pregnancy risks. Over 1,300 articles on smoking and health risks were published in various science and medical journals during the same five-year period.

Besides affecting what is written about their products and the dangers of smoking, the tobacco industry has other ways of gaining legitimacy and deflecting criticism. Sponsorships are one such method. By sponsoring a respected event or institution, they buy their way into our culture.

Tobacco companies have sponsored the American Ballet Theatre, the Dance Theatre of Harlem, and the Joffrey Ballet.

Some specific examples of sponsored events are the Arts Festival of Atlanta, the More Fashion Awards, the Virginia Slims tennis tournaments, and the Kool Jazz Festivals, to name just a few.

They have given money to the Sierra Club
for Earth Day; to various states for their state fairs;
and to family and children's events like the Great
July 4th Festival and the Avenue of the Americas
Family Expo, both held in New York.

The Kool Achiever Awards recognized civic
leaders in collaboration with the National Urban
League, Inc.; the National Publishers Association;
and the NAACP.

Many women's organizations have accepted
money offered by the cigarette industry. Some of
these groups include the
National Women's Political
Caucus, the Women's Cam-
paign Fund, the Women's
Research and Educational
Institute (an affiliate of the Congressional Caucus
on Women's Issues), the League of Women Voters
Education Fund, Women Executives in State

*Philip Morris declared
operating revenues of
over 49 billion dollars
in 2000 from domestic
and international
cigarette sales.*

Government, and the American Federation of Business and Professional Women's Clubs.

Minority women's groups have also been recipients of tobacco-company funding. Some of these include the National Coalition of 100 Black Women, U.S. Hispanic Women's Chamber of Commerce, and the Asian Pacific American Women's Leadership Institute. Other minority beneficiaries include the United Negro College Fund and the National Hispanic College Fund.

Philip Morris worked with several large corporations and women's advocacy groups to form a coalition called Safe@Work, an antistalking organization. They also partnered with the

Philip Morris is the largest cigarette manu-facturer. They have captured over 50 percent of the market.

National Network to End Domestic Violence Fund to create a foundation called Doors of Hope, through which grants are provided to organizations around the country that fight domestic violence.

The results of all of these sponsorships are somewhat predictable. The Congressional Caucus on Women's Issues introduced the Women's Health Equity Act, which included six bills on disease prevention, none of which mentioned smoking.

The National Black Monitor, a newspaper insert included in 80 monthly newspapers targeted to blacks, ran an article asking readers to oppose anti-tobacco legislation. They were asked to view such legislation as discrimination against "this industry which has befriended us, often far more than any other, in our hour of greatest need." They must not be looking too closely at the numbers of their brethren who are felled each year by smoking. If the tobacco industry can be called a friend, it is certainly a dangerous one to have.

Auto racing provides another popular venue for cigarette advertising. The NASCAR Winston Cup and Marlboro Grand Prix are just two tobacco-industry sponsored events. If you've ever watched one of these shows, you've seen tobacco-brand logos splashed everywhere. A certain air of legitimacy comes with sharing logo space with other large and nationally recognized companies.

Advertising dollars spent on marketing long and ultra-long cigarettes, which are targeted primarily to women, increased from 29 percent in 1975 to 40 percent in 1998. The market share (how many people use a particular product) saw a similar increase. It went from 25 percent in 1975, to 40 percent in 1998. This would have made the advertisers very happy since it was proof to their clients that what they were doing was working.

There have been a number of cigarette brands developed for and targeted to women. The cigarette designers seem to focus on the "slim" theme more often with women's cigarettes. This appears to be an intentional attempt, even if by only using word association, to make smoking even more attractive to women who may be concerned with their weight.

A few years ago, there was an R.J. Reynolds brand (Dakota) in development that was heavily researched and specifically targeted to young, low-income, less well-educated women. These target consumers supposedly had no career prospects beyond high school.

Dakota sales never did take off. Maybe it was because their marketing plan was too narrowly focused to be successful. But when this highly targeted scheme came to light after an insider leaked it to the press, R.J. Reynolds altered its strategy, which resulted in reduced sales that eventually led the company to withdraw the product. This was after spending more than $1.5 million on market research and development alone.

Advertising directed toward women can be particularly manipulative. They try to connect women's issues like empowerment, independence, and individuality with the use of cigarettes, a product known to be highly addictive. And they do this with such impunity that it borders on being scandalous.

The recent campaign for Virginia Slims tells women to "Find Your Voice." It's hard to tell if the ad executives are being intentionally callous or if they are just completely missing the irony. So many women have lost their voices to mouth, throat, and lung cancer, and so many others have lost their very lives, because they were drawn into the illusion painted by the cigarette industry and became captive smokers.

Having movie stars and cartoon characters smoke onscreen is another way we get the message that smoking is common, desirable, and socially acceptable. It is no longer legal for the tobacco companies to directly pay for this kind of exposure, but it's too late; smoking has already become a commonplace image on the big screen, with some characters being defined by the presence of a cigarette, pipe, or cigar. Famous actors and actresses who smoke are sending a very powerful message to their young and impressionable fans.

Advertising tends to distract us from the seriousness of smoking by using beautiful images to make it all seem so benign. Think of the sunset scenes of cowboys on their horses and the laughing friends showing how alive they are with pleasure. We are being driven to associate smoking with some of life's more beautiful moments. Advertisers know their business, and they do it very well.

We need to show the cigarette industry that their days are numbered. No matter how illusory their advertising is, we will not be taken in.

We've found our voice, thank you, and we say "The game is over. We quit."

REALITIES OF QUITTING

There have been a few studies showing that women may have a tougher time quitting than men. But the results are inconsistent, and we cannot draw any conclusions until there is consensus among researchers in this area. In the meantime, this chapter contains some information that may be helpful to you if you are a woman struggling to quit smoking.

First of all, you should know that former smokers take an average of 18.6 years to quit smoking and make 10.8 attempts before they are finally successful. Of those who have successfully quit smoking, 88.1 percent stopped cold turkey.

Some evidence suggests that women may experience worse withdrawal symptoms in the days before and during their periods. Variables like the presence and severity of PMS symptoms can also play a part. Women who experience menstrual distress are somewhat more likely to suffer severe withdrawal symptoms. It may be better for some women to plan a quit attempt right after menstruation, rather than right before or during it.

You may have heard a statistic in the past that said that when people quit smoking, one-third of them gain weight, one-third of them lose it, and the rest of the people can expect to see no change. This has been found to be untrue among women, something you probably already suspected if you're a woman and you've tried to quit smoking before.

Women show a typical weight gain of about 6 to 12 pounds in the first year of smoking cessation, according to the Surgeon General's report. This should not alarm you, since the good news is that it stabilizes and even declines after that. And the waist-to-hip ratio starts to lose its more masculine pattern over time as well.

Statistics show that weight gain is not a predictor of relapse. Just because you gain weight does not mean that you will have trouble staying off cigarettes. In fact, two studies showed that those who gained the most weight during the early stages of quitting were more likely to have lasting success.

And one recent study showed that the women who were least concerned about gaining weight actually gained the least amount of weight. This was possibly because they were less likely to engage in unhealthy eating habits, such as skipping meals, in order to control weight.

Another point to keep in mind is that surveys have shown that smokers are more likely to see themselves as overweight, even if their weight falls within the normal range.

Hopefully, gaining a little weight is much less scary for you than the fear of losing your future to a premature death. The negative health consequences of moderate weight gain simply pale in comparison to the terrible effects of continuing to smoke.

The following are some predictors of success in smoking cessation:

– smokes fewer than 10 cigarettes a day

– is confident in ability to quit

– has a partner who doesn't smoke

– breastfeeds longer than six months

– started smoking at an older age

– first tried to quit at a younger age

– is unconcerned about gaining weight

– has made frequent attempts to quit

– has a high expectation of not smoking
  in the future

It is not necessary for all or even most of these factors to be present for a quitter to be successful. Being a heavy smoker or living with a partner who smokes does statistically point to a greater likelihood of relapse, but we are not statistics and every-one is different. You may well have other more significant factors in your life that will help predict success for you.

Almost 40 percent of current smokers have tried to quit in the past year.

Do what you can to tip the odds in your favor, and then trust in your ability to make it happen. Your belief in yourself and your commitment to change are the strongest predictors of all.

Part Five

Staying With It

TIPS FROM EX-SMOKERS

By now you may have listened to the *Give It Up!*
CD a few times. You may even be well on your way
to becoming an ex-smoker for good.

One thing to keep in mind is that the whole
business of becoming an ex-smoker is a process, and
not an overnight one at that. You begin by removing
the cigarettes and not smoking anymore. After a
short while, the physical addiction and cravings
start to leave. Finally, you plateau and reach the

maintenance stage. But to get to this point, you must work on the triggers, the things that make you want to break down and have a cigarette.

Distraction works very well. It can get you past the point of desperation and back to the calm resolve you need to remain clean. Your feelings of vulnerability may last for a few minutes, for several days, or for even longer if you are going through a stressful period in your life.

Reinforcement is another valuable tool for avoiding a relapse. You want to remind yourself of the wonderful gifts you are getting by remaining smoke-free. It can be easy to forget why you quit if you are having a bad day and all you can think of is how a cigarette could calm you down and make you feel better.

Lung cancer is the number-one cancer, accounting for over 25 percent of all deaths from cancer.

Your body's memory of the pleasures of smoking can push its way up into your consciousness, sometimes when you least expect it. It says "Hello. Remember me? Wouldn't you like to get to know me again?" So you must be on guard and prepared with an answer. Yes, you remember how you had trouble breathing and had a cough. You remember how awful it felt to be trapped in your addiction. You remember the stink and the stigma that surrounded you.

Sometimes quitting smoking can be a moment-by-moment struggle. It has been described by many ex-smokers as the most difficult thing they ever had to do.

The following tips are from people who have quit and stayed quit. You may think some of these tips sound silly and you may have already tried others. But remember, every attempt to quit is a fresh one, so don't be too quick to dismiss any particular idea. It just might be the one that helps you get through it this time.

- Drink a big glass of water.

- Take a brisk walk.

- Suck on a lollipop or cinnamon stick.

- Write your feelings down.

- Stick a toothpick in your mouth.

- Put your nose in some flowers and inhale.

- Repeat a prayer in your head.

- Rub some mint on your wrist and smell it.

- Light a match and blow it out.

- Chew some sugarless gum or eat a mint.

- Take a deep breath and hold it, then
  exhale like you're breathing out smoke.

- Roll your shoulders, loosen up, stretch.

- Eat an orange or some celery sticks.
  Keep various fruits and veggies handy.

- Breathe in slowly through your nose;
  exhale slowly through your mouth.

- Brush teeth. Floss. Rinse out your mouth.

- Visualize your lungs taking in oxygen.

- Take a two-inch-square sticky note or other small piece of paper, and roll it up like a cigarette. Now hold it, puff through it, and marvel at the absurdity of it all.
- Tell your friends about how you quit smoking. When you have others cheering you on, you are more likely to get through the rough times.
- Think about how you'll feel tomorrow if you give in versus if you stay clean.

You may have noticed that there are quite a few oral tips listed. Smoking was a very oral experience for you, and it was carried out many times each day. It's okay to pay extra attention to your mouth for a while. You are retraining your body, giving it new behaviors to learn and latch onto. Remember, you are doing whatever it takes. Even if you find yourself addicted to lollipops or chocolate for a while, getting a few extra cavities or gaining a little weight is far less dangerous to your overall health than is getting cancer or emphysema.

Another tool is to write down all of the reasons you want to smoke, then list all of the reasons you don't. Repetition is very helpful here, so do it each time you're struggling, not just once.

Remember, the struggle won't last forever. You will notice that you think about smoking less and less often as each day passes. Give yourself time. It gets better. Much better.

You may have some ideas of your own. Jot them down, and refer to them often. Please feel free to copy these list pages as often as you wish.

———

My personal tricks for getting past a craving:

_____

_____

_____

_____

_____

_____

_____

_____

_____

_____

_____

_____

Why I want a cigarette right at this moment:

_____

_____

_____

_____

_____

_____

_____

_____

_____

_____

_____

_____

Why I don't ever want to be a smoker again:

_____

_____

_____

_____

_____

_____

_____

_____

_____

_____

_____

_____

_____

_____

_____

_____

_____

_____

_____

_____

_____

_____

_____

_____

_____

_____

IT ALL ADDS UP

There are many fascinating and terrible facts surrounding smoking and its consequences. There are also some very interesting financial numbers that help explain why it is such a huge business and why it won't go away overnight.

You might skim through these if you ever feel your resolve slipping. They ought to help perk your motivation right back up again. They may look familiar to you since they are a compilation of the sidebar copy blocks sprinkled throughout this book. Grouping them together in one spot makes them a little easier for you to review and ponder.

- 88 percent of adult smokers tried their first cigarette before age 18.

- The younger you are when you start smoking, the more likely you are to become addicted and to be a heavy smoker later in life. You are also more likely to die prematurely than a smoker who starts smoking later in life.

- 7 people every minute throughout the world die from a tobacco-related illness (that's 4 million this year).

- 50 percent of current smokers will die from a smoking-related illness.

- Spending on tobacco advertising went from 6.73 billion dollars in 1998 to 8.24 billion dollars in 1999.

- 75 percent of smokers say they want to quit.

- Approximately 3 out of 4 people do not smoke.

- On any given day in the U.S., over 450 people will receive a diagnosis of lung cancer.

- In 1994, tobacco companies listed 599 ingredients they routinely added to cigarettes. This disclosure was in response to a U.S. Food and Drug Administration directive.

- Almost half of the world's children breathe second-hand smoke.

- The total annual economic burden of cigarette smoking in the U.S. may exceed 135 billion dollars.

- 90 percent of lung cancer deaths are attributed to smoking.

- 88 percent of successful ex-smokers quit cold turkey.

- 8 nonsmokers will die of lung cancer today because they were exposed to second-hand smoke.

- Almost half of all people who have ever smoked have quit smoking.

- An average of 14 years of life is lost for every woman who dies from smoking.

- The five-year survival rate for lung cancer
  is about 13 percent. This means 87 percent of
  those diagnosed with lung cancer will die within
  five years, some within weeks.

- A 1998 survey found that almost 65 percent
  of high school seniors prefer to date someone
  who doesn't smoke.

- The three most heavily advertised cigarette
  brands are also the three top-selling brands.
  These are Marlboro, Camel, and Newport.

- Children and teens who try to quit report the
  same withdrawal symptoms as adults and have
  the same problems with relapse.

- Almost 40 percent of current smokers have
  tried to quit in the past year.

- About one-third of women who quit smoking during pregnancy are still abstinent one year after giving birth.

- The World Health Organization predicts that if smoking prevalence continues to increase at the current rate, the annual number of tobacco-related deaths will reach 10 million by 2030.

- Philip Morris declared operating revenues of over 49 billion dollars in 2000 from domestic and international cigarette sales.

- Philip Morris is the largest cigarette manufacturer. They have captured over 50 percent of the market.

• Lung cancer is the number-one cancer,
  accounting for over 25 percent of all deaths
  from cancer.

Once you become an ex-smoker, you will help influence others around you to quit too. Then maybe someday these statistics won't be so dramatic.

IN CLOSING

By now you might be feeling rather saddened or even angered by some of the things you just read. This would be a good thing, since both the emotions and the intellect need to be engaged in order to effect change. Your entire being has to participate.

Turn on the CD and continue listening to the stories. They will inspire you to keep moving toward your new life of freedom. Listen repeatedly to help really drive it home.

The groundwork has been laid, but the path is not without peril. You will need to work on that ego of yours to keep it from taking back the reins. Remind yourself that you are smart enough to quit smoking, that you are not alone, and that you can tap into your higher self for help at any time.

That little voice begging you to quit will never leave you alone, you know. You might as well heed its demands. So give it up now and stop smoking for life. *Your life.* Don't waste another day. Give it up so you can live it up!

———

Greg's father passed away shortly
before this book was going to press.
He will be sadly missed by his family,
especially his grandchildren.

———

Join other readers online, and share your successful quitting experience. Your story may inspire someone else to take this momentous step toward a longer, healthier life. Or visit to get a little inspiration for yourself.

The author is collecting stories and input for possible future writings. Do you feel this book and CD was successful for you? You are encouraged to contribute your thoughts and opinions.

Visit www.lovetogiveitup.com.

———

RECOMMENDED READING

Cigarettes: What the Warning Label
Doesn't Tell You

Dr. Elizabeth Whelan and The American
Council on Science and Health, 1996

How We Die, Reflections on Life's Final Chapter
Sherwin B. Nuland, 1993

Marketing Cigarettes to Women
The Surgeon General's Report:
Women and Smoking
May 2001

The Last Puff: Ex-Smokers Share the Secrets
of Their Success
Gene A. Spiller (Contributor),
John W. Farquhar, 1991

WEB SITES OF INTEREST

Action on Smoking and Health

> http://www.ash.org

American Cancer Society

> http://www.cancer.org

American Council on Science and Health

> http://www.acsh.org/tobacco

American Lung Association

> http://www.lungusa.org

BMJ Publishing Group, TC Online

> http://tobaccocontrol.com

CancerSource.com

> http://cancersource.com

Centers for Disease Control

http://www.cdc.gov/tobacco

Health Scout

http://www.healthscout.com

(Search for keyword: Smoking)

National Center for Tobacco-Free Kids

http://tobaccofreekids.org

National Women's Health Information Center

http://www.4woman.gov/quitsmoking

Olivija's COPD Resources

http://www.olivija.com/

and

http://www.megalink.net/~dale/olivija4.html

(Includes pictures of diseased lungs)

The Truth

>   http://thetruth.com

Tobacco BBS

>   http://www.tobacco.org

University of Utah

>   http://telpath2.med.utah.eduWebPath/
>
>   LUNGHTML/LUNG068.html
>
>   *(Includes pictures of diseased lungs)*

U.S. Surgeon General

>   http://www.surgeongeneral.gov

Washington DOC (Doctors Ought to Care)

>   http://www.kickbutt.org

World Health Organization

>   http://tobacco.who.int

REFERENCES

American Cancer Society, Inc.

- *Freshstart program materials*
- *Cancer Facts & Figures,* 2001

American Heart Association
- *Pro-Oxidant Effect of Vitamin E in
  Cigarette Smokers Consuming a High
  Polyunsaturated Fat Diet*
  Richard B. Weinberg; Barbara S.
  VanderWerken; Rachel A. Anderson;
  Jane E. Stegner; Michael J. Thomas,
  study published in *Arteriosclerosis,
  Thrombosis, and Vascular Biology,* 2001

Centers for Disease Control
- *Morbidity and Mortality Weekly Report*
  May 25, 2001 / Vol. 50 / No. 20
- CDC Web site: http://www.cdc.gov/tobacco

Henningfield, J.E., and R.M Keenan
- *Nicotine delivery kinetics and abuse
  liability,* study published in *Journal of
  Consulting & Clinical Psychology,* 1993

REFERENCES

International Consultation on Tobacco and Youth
- *What in the World Works?*
Singapore, 1999

Levine, Michele
- Study on smoking and weight gain
*Journal of Consulting and Clinical
Psychology,* August 2001

National Cancer Institute/National Institutes
of Health
- *Smoking and Tobacco Control
Monograph No. 10,* 1999

National Library of Medicine
- *Cigarette smoking and attention:
processing speed or specific effects?*
Mancuso G, Lejeune M, Ansseau M.
Psychopharmacology, June 2001

- *Tobacco lobby political influence on
U.S. state legislatures in the 1990s*
Givel MS, Glantz SA
Tobacco Control, June 2001

REFERENCES

National Women's Health Information Center
- *Many teens underestimate smoking risks: survey*
Charnicia E. Huggins
Journal of Adolescent Health, 2001

- *Smoking may kill off women's eggs: study*
Amy Norton
Nature Genetics, 2001

Parrot, Andy C.
- Study on smoking and stress
American Psychologist, October 1999

Philip Morris Companies Inc.
- *Annual Report,* 2000

Surgeon General's Reports
- *Reducing Tobacco Use,* 2000
- *Women and Smoking,* 2001

REFERENCES

U.S. Public Health Service
- *Treating Tobacco Use and Dependence*
Summary, June 2000

World Health Organization
- WHO Web site:
http://tobacco.who.int
- *Tobacco & The Rights Of The Child*
Report, 2001

———

INDEX

abruptio placentae   102

addiction   2, 4, 6-7, 19-20, 23, 55-56, 60, 62-63, 67-69, 94, 101, 125, 127

advertising   14-15, 21, 87-88, 105-106, 110-111, 113-114, 137

alcohol   2, 70, 91-92, 100

amphetamine   20

antioxidant   31

anxiety disorders   100

attention deficit disorder   100

auditory   10, 80

auto racing   110

behavior   38, 54-55, 92, 129

belief   77-78, 121

benefits   47, 49, 51

binge   92, 94

binge drinking   92

birth defects   36

blood pressure   32, 49

breast cancer   88

breastfeeding   4, 120

bronchitis   37, 40, 82

bulimia   100

caffeine   70

calcium   35

INDEX

carbon dioxide   61

carbon monoxide   33, 49, 62, 103

cartoon characters   113

cataracts   39

cerebrovascular disease   40

chemicals   17, 19, 34, 37, 103

children   15, 37, 80, 92, 95, 104, 108, 137, 139

chocolate   5, 70, 129

choice   15-16, 19, 55, 60, 64, 97

cilia   47-48, 50

circulation   41, 48, 50

cleft palate   104

cocaine   20

cold turkey   54, 69, 118, 138

collagen   30

college   81, 90, 109

colon cancer   6

congenital malformations   104

coronary heart disease   50-51

courage   58

craving   4, 16, 20, 67-68, 74, 125, 131

dentist   31, 71

depression   40, 91, 100

detox   4, 71

diabetes mellitus   41

diet   30, 72, 91, 153

drugs   91

ear infections   37, 40

economic burden   38, 138

ectopic pregnancy   100, 102

education   xi, 22, 90, 104, 108

ego   54-57, 59, 144

emotion   10, 60, 77-78, 143

emphysema   6-7, 40, 130

empowerment   87, 113

endorphins   71

environmental toxins   37

estrogen   35-36

exercise   4, 60, 71-72, 79

eye disease   40

father   82, 91, 103

fertility   36, 41

fetal death   104

free radicals   29

gastrointestinal disease   37

gateway drug   92

genetic   103

gingivitis   40

gum disease   31

headaches   40, 48

healing   36, 75

hearing loss   40

INDEX

heart disease   36, 40, 50-51, 107

heavy smoker   15, 30, 121, 136

high blood pressure   40

high school seniors   91, 139

higher self   54, 56-57, 59, 67, 144

hip fracture   35, 100

hypnotherapy   4, 6

immunological deficiencies   41

impotence   36, 41

incontinence   41

infertility   41

influenza   41

insulin resistance   41

leukemia   41

low birth weight   38, 103

lower-income bracket   23

lung cancer   6, 14, 19, 41-42, 51, 57, 75, 88, 107, 113, 126, 137-139, 141

magazine-publishing industry   21

marijuana   91-92

market research   112

market share   111

media   87-88

menopause   36, 40, 87

menstrual distress   118

metabolism   33

miscarriage   36, 41, 100, 102

mood-altering   70

motivate   77

movie   5, 14, 113

movie stars   14, 113

music   ix, 10

nicotine   4, 17-20, 24, 30, 62, 69-70, 101, 103, 153

osteoporosis   35, 40-41

oxygen   5, 26, 33, 36-37, 48, 61-62, 74, 103, 128

paternal smoking   104

peptic ulcer disease   41

periodontal disease   41

placenta previa   102

PMS   118

pneumonia   41

polyunsaturated fats   30

prayer   4, 57, 128

predictors   90, 120-121

pregnancy   3, 87, 91, 101-104, 107, 140

premature wrinkling   41

pro-oxidant   31

promotions   105

psoriasis   41

relapse   75, 95, 119, 121, 126, 139

respiratory illnesses   99

revenue   106, 108, 140

rheumatoid arthritis   100

INDEX

role model   21, 64

sales   105, 108, 112, 140

schizophrenia   100

second-hand smoke   37, 57, 103, 137-138

self-esteem   59, 60, 90

self-image   25

serenity   54, 58

sibling   82, 91, 94

sinus congestion   50

sperm count   36

spiritual   26, 60

sponsorships   107, 110

stillbirth   38, 103

stress   16, 24, 72, 74, 77, 126, 155

stroke   42, 50

subconscious   55, 78

Sudden Infant Death Syndrome   38, 103

support group   69

Surgeon General   88, 119, 147, 151, 155

survivor   76

tar   35

taste   40, 48

teens   x, 7, 25, 38, 78, 83, 91-92, 97, 139, 155

tobacco industry   21, 105, 107, 111

toxin   32, 37

ultra-long cigarettes   111

INDEX

vitamin deficiency   30

vitamins A, B, C, and E   30

waist-to-hip ratio   35, 119

weight   24, 73, 87, 91, 112, 118-120, 130, 154

withdrawal   70, 74, 95, 118, 139

women's magazines   106

wrinkles   29, 41

Send a copy of **Give It Up!** to a friend or loved one.

O R D E R   F O R M

– **Fax orders:** Fax this completed form to 303.670.4459.
– **Telephone orders:** Call 1.866.GiveItUp (1.866.448.3488).
   Please have your credit card ready.
– **E-mail orders:** amitchell@alyeskapress.com.
– **Postal orders:** Alyeska Press, LLC, 1153 Bergen Parkway, Suite M,
   PMB #275, Evergreen, CO 80439.
– **Online orders:** www.lovetogiveitup.com.

Prices subject to change without notice.

Please send me **Give It Up! Stop smoking for life.** I understand that
I may return it for a full refund at any time, for any reason.

Name: _____

Address: _____

City: _____ State: _____ ZIP: _____

Telephone: _____

E-mail (optional): _____

Payment: ☐ Check or money order enclosed
                ☐ Credit card:
                    ☐ VISA   ☐ Mastercard

Credit card number: _____

Expiration date: _____

Name on card: _____

Signature: _____

– Number of book/CD sets _____ x $19.95 ea.   = $ _____

– Subtract discount for multiple orders*   – $ _____

– Add 4.2% sales tax if shipping to a Colorado address
                                    + $ _____

– Add shipping** (see below)   + $ _____

Total   = $ _____

*Discounts for nonbookstore customers as follows:
Book/CD sets 2 through 3: 10%, book/CD sets 4 through 199: 40%.
For quantities over 200 please see info at www.lovetogiveitup.com.

**Shipping:
U.S. destinations: Add $4.50 for first two book/CD sets, $2 for each
additional book/CD set. **International destinations:** Add $9 for first
book/CD set, $5 for each additional book/CD set.

Send a copy of **Give It Up!** to a friend or loved one.

O R D E R   F O R M

- **Fax orders:** Fax this completed form to 303.670.4459.
- **Telephone orders:** Call 1.866.GiveItUp (1.866.448.3488).
  Please have your credit card ready.
- **E-mail orders:** amitchell@alyeskapress.com.
- **Postal orders:** Alyeska Press, LLC, 1153 Bergen Parkway, Suite M,
  PMB #275, Evergreen, CO 80439.
- **Online orders:** www.lovetogiveitup.com.

Prices subject to change without notice.

Please send me **Give It Up! Stop smoking for life.** I understand that
I may return it for a full refund at any time, for any reason.

Name: _____

Address: _____

City: _____ State: _____ ZIP: _____

Telephone: _____

E-mail (optional): _____

Payment: ☐ Check or money order enclosed
                     ☐ Credit card:
                              ☐ VISA   ☐ Mastercard

Credit card number: _____

Expiration date: _____

Name on card: _____

Signature: _____

– Number of book/CD sets _____ x $19.95 ea.   = $ _____

– Subtract discount for multiple orders*   – $ _____

– Add 4.2% sales tax if shipping to a Colorado address
                                                  + $ _____

– Add shipping** (see below)   + $ _____

Total   = $ _____

*Discounts for nonbookstore customers as follows:
Book/CD sets 2 through 3: 10%, book/CD sets 4 through 199: 40%.
For quantities over 200 please see info at www.lovetogiveitup.com.

**Shipping:
U.S. destinations: Add $4.50 for first two book/CD sets, $2 for each
additional book/CD set. **International destinations:** Add $9 for first
book/CD set, $5 for each additional book/CD set.

Send a copy of **Give It Up!** to a friend or loved one.

O R D E R F O R M

- **Fax orders:** Fax this completed form to 303.670.4459.
- **Telephone orders:** Call 1.866.GiveItUp (1.866.448.3488).
  Please have your credit card ready.
- **E-mail orders:** amitchell@alyeskapress.com.
- **Postal orders:** Alyeska Press, LLC, 1153 Bergen Parkway, Suite M,
  PMB #275, Evergreen, CO 80439.
- **Online orders:** www.lovetogiveitup.com.

Prices subject to change without notice.

Please send me **Give It Up! Stop smoking for life.** I understand that
I may return it for a full refund at any time, for any reason.

Name: _____

Address: _____

City: _____ State: _____ ZIP: _____

Telephone: _____

E-mail (optional): _____

Payment: ☐ Check or money order enclosed
                ☐ Credit card:
                        ☐ VISA   ☐ Mastercard

Credit card number: _____

Expiration date: _____

Name on card: _____

Signature: _____

– Number of book/CD sets _____ x $19.95 ea.   = $ _____

– Subtract discount for multiple orders*   – $ _____

– Add 4.2% sales tax if shipping to a Colorado address
                                                 + $ _____

– Add shipping** (see below)   + $ _____

Total   = $ _____

*Discounts for nonbookstore customers as follows:
Book/CD sets 2 through 3: 10%, book/CD sets 4 through 199: 40%.
For quantities over 200 please see info at www.lovetogiveitup.com.

** Shipping:
U.S. destinations: Add $4.50 for first two book/CD sets, $2 for each
additional book/CD set. **International destinations:** Add $9 for first
book/CD set, $5 for each additional book/CD set.